CONCRETE CONFIDENCE

HOW TO ACQUIRE THE CONFIDENCE TO MONETIZE ANY INDUSTRY

JANE WILEY

TABLE OF CONTENT

INTRODUCTION

Today, the term "monetization" has a new meaning. People are attempting to make money from just about anything during these trying times. Some people are hitting the jackpot by generating multiple revenue streams from a single product. While others are merely wasting away, struggling to comprehend the idea of monetization,

You can learn how to monetize things by reading this eBook.how to increase your income with little effort and ensure that it continues to flow into your bank account.

CHAPTER ONE

The Rules of the Game

If you look up what monetization is on the Internet, you will find a lot of different definitions. There are a lot of different things that fall under the umbrella term "monetization," but we can pretty much say that "monetization" means making money out of things that most people don't usually think are worth money. You have monetized the collection, for instance, if you have an old collection of Archie Comics from your dad or uncle and can sell them for a substantial sum.

Monetization is the process of making money in unexpected ways from ordinary things.

It's easy to see why people are putting everything they have at risk to make money from everything they see. or even hide from view.

People are making money with their unique abilities. You are monetizing your talent if you use your special aptitude for math to tutor the neighbor's child for money. Your writing talent can be monetized by selling a piece of content you have written.

We are all very aware of how to make money, but we probably have never done it systematically. Our jobs pay us, and most of the time, we are content with what we get and don't try to make much money. However, it is essential to know that there are several additional sources of income. We can enjoy the influx of cash for the rest of our lives and generate streams of passive income through things we set up once if we play our cards right. That would be something along the lines of product royalties.

Monetization is the ability to earn money outside of your usual occupation. Your effort matters, not the value of the product. It's about figuring out whether or not a skill or thing can be made money, and then how to do it.

We are going to look at several different ways that you can create income streams for yourself out of things that you never thought you could make money from.

CHAPTER TWO

Making Money Out of Anything...

Anything first thing you need to know if you want to have the self-assurance to make money out of anything is that you can!

But what exactly is this "anything" about? You might have invented a product. You can make money if it has a utility—and sometimes even if it doesn't. Or, it could be a product that you've bought from someone else and are now allowed to sell. Alternately, it could be a skill you possess. It could simply be your knowledge or specialized expertise in a particular area.

There are numerous opportunities for earning money even for those who believe they have nothing. Here, no one is wasting space.

Let us talk about something very, very positive before diving headfirst into discussions about how you can accomplish this. The Secret of Success. This law, which has taken the world by storm, has a lot to say about our topic. In a nutshell, the law states that the entire universe aligns to fulfill your desire when you think about it strongly. Yes, the law says that thoughts make things happen. It talks about mental energy, which can cause things to happen.

People who have said that the law is nonsense and doesn't work for them

started in disbelief because this is a very real law. You must have complete faith in the law if you want it to work. Concentrate solely on your goal.

Consider what you want. Without hesitation or hesitation, think. Things will begin to happen gradually. You will undoubtedly take action in that direction when you think deeply. That single objective will be the focus of everything you do.

Naturally, things will begin to progress. You will get closer to achieving your goals if you think deeply and consistently.

You must comply with this law even if you intend to monetize something.

You must never, ever think that there is no money in this. Consider the bigger picture rather than just the dollar amount. As a side note, the money comes in. It doesn't take long for you to be rewarded financially if you put in your time and effort.

CHAPTER THREE

Why You Can't Forget the Internet

Today, online businesses and monetization are almost synonymous.

The Internet will be the first and most important activity for people who want to make money from anything. They use online resources to make money for a variety of reasons.

First and foremost, monetization as a whole has evolved. People are no longer thinking traditionally. They

are putting their creative juices to use to generate income from novel concepts and ideas. This cannot be accomplished unless these business owners can locate customers who are interested in what they are selling. To put it succinctly, they operate in specialized niches, which necessitates the identification of individuals who can be considered their niche customers.

That is allowed by the Internet. When you're working online, there are a lot of different ways to find people who are interested in what you're trying to do. Do you want to create a fan site for a show that no one in your immediate vicinity watches? That can be accomplished online. Do you want to talk about a

pastime you think no one else does? On the Internet, you will be surprised at how many people share your special affection. Do you believe that no one is interested in your particular skill? You can find a plethora of people who do on the internet. Or, more likely, you've created a product that no one in your circle finds useful. You will be pleasantly surprised to learn that there is also a niche market online for that product.

The most important thing is how the Internet makes you feel better. You gain confidence in creating that object or conceptualizing that idea and monetizing it when you realize that several people share your

interests and are also interested in what you are trying to sell.

The fact that there is no rejection is the best part. The days when sellers had to sell to customers are long gone; Bringing interested customers to your door is now very much possible thanks to the Internet. The Internet is a great place to market yourself if you're the shy, introverted type who cringes at the thought of not being accepted.

The biggest draw, of course, is the vast array of online resources. You can get people to come right to your door so they can buy whatever it is you're selling. Even if it does nothing else for you, this is what boosts your confidence and motivates you to keep going with your business.

CHAPTER FOUR

Create something popular and successful that you can use as a vehicle for monetization as your first step.

The numerous fan sites that have resulted from American Idol are well-known to almost everyone who is a fan. The majority of these websites were initially nothing more than fan sites with no money involved. However, as their popularity grew, their creators began to believe that they could also make money from them, which

led to the development of a vast monetization option.

The Harry Potter series experienced the same thing. One of the almost-official Harry Potter fan sites, Mugglenet.com, didn't start out making money. It was merely a gathering place for fans of the wizarding world to learn more about him. However, once its popularity increased to an astonishing level, it became obvious that it could be monetized.

In both of these instances, individuals first constructed something without even considering financial gain, then made those items popular and began making money from them. This indicates that you do not necessarily need to

start making money from the beginning. You could even go in later and use what you have to make money. To monetize a product, all it takes is for it to become extremely popular.

It is not difficult to make something extremely popular on the Internet. Blogs are a useful tool at your disposal. Create a popular blog using either Wordpress.com or Blogger.com, two free blogging platforms. You can begin monetizing your blog in a variety of ways once it reaches a certain level of popularity—that is, when a large number of people visit it—such as by selling eBooks through it, subscriptions to newsletters, or even eventually creating a

membership site. You could investigate monetizing streams through options like social networking. By creating communities, inviting people to join them, and providing them with useful information, your business—it's about time we started calling it a business—will gain popularity. Numerous opportunities to earn money open up for you as soon as people start coming in.

CHAPTER FIVE

Goodwill Hunting and Finding Niches

You have begun your journey toward monetization. Now, you need people who are willing to pay you.

Anything you try to monetize will be very difficult if you don't target the right people. After all, if you don't find people who are willing to spend money to learn your recipes, how could you possibly make money from them? You see where I'm going with this: you have to find your niche.

On the Internet, Search Engine Optimization, or SEO for short, is one of the most effective methods

for accomplishing this. If you're just starting with online businesses, you probably already know a little bit about SEO. If you don't, the meaning is as follows: SEO simply refers to optimizing your website—a blog is also considered a website—for search engines. Because people use search engines to find information, this is extremely significant. When someone wants to learn more about something, they use a search engine like Google or Yahoo! to type in a word or phrase. or Ask. After that, they click on the links that appear. Most of the time, people only click on the links on the first page, and few even go to the second page. As a result, appearing on the first page of any search engine becomes extremely important for anyone who wants to become famous on the Internet and, consequently, monetize something.

You can build a large fan base on the blogs and forums of other people even if you don't have a website of your own. Numerous blog commentators cultivate their fan bases by receiving a large number of responses. When they gain such a following, they immediately start their blogs or websites and introduce themselves to these individuals. Without putting in any money of your own, this could be a great way to find your niche and gain their trust.

Article marketing is another method. You could write articles about the

topic you want to make money from. After that, these articles could be published on sites like EzineArticles.com, iSnare.com, ArticleAlley.com, GoArticles.com, ArticleCity.com, and so forth. The fact that these sites are already popular with search engines is the best part about submitting your articles to them. As a result, if you submit some very instructive articles to this site, you might attract a large following of fans. Also, keep in mind that your articles will be found by people who are looking for information about that particular area.

CHAPTER SIX

Promoting Your Content Online:

When Will You Feel Confidence?

When you are confident in what you are selling, you can only make money.

Even a fruit seller needs to be convinced of the quality of his oranges or nobody will buy them from him. However, you are certain to play with greater stakes than just oranges here.

Confidence is one of the most important things you need to sell anything. That is what you are

looking for. But when does self-assurance arrive?

You may have confidence from the beginning. When you look at a particular short story you've written or a video you've made showing how to make bouillabaisse in a particular way, you might feel pretty confident that you can make money from it. You can, and there are a few options for doing so.

Although confidence begins here, there is still a long way to go.

The most important thing to understand here is that initial confidence does not last. The consolidation of your confidence is what matters. It must be bolstered.

And what bolsters your self-assurance? Results are what matter.

Your confidence starts to grow when you can see that things are actually transpiring in the manner in which you would like them to, and when you can see that you are actually receiving the money that you had originally intended to receive.

However, it's not just about money. Any kind of result could help you keep moving forward. Even a small comment on a blog post or article that someone has written can give some people the motivation they need to keep going. Give it a shot. Post something to your blog about a subject that interests you. If you receive a response for that, you are aware that someone was influenced in some way by your comment. It gives you the boost you need to work more effectively.

It could be anything that inspires you or leads to something. It could be more people visiting your blog, people commenting on it, someone inviting you to a social networking group, someone emailing you, someone directly asking you something about your expertise, or any number of other possibilities. Or, most importantly, and perhaps most importantly of all, it could be someone who actually buys what you're trying to sell and pays you.

Your confidence will really grow as a result of this. However, you must keep in mind that you must begin

with some confidence. The ideal situation would be to have unwavering confidence from the start, but if that doesn't seem to be the case, you could at least find inspiration in the successes that keep coming your way.

CHAPTER SEVEN

The Power of Viral Marketing

Nothing boosts an entrepreneur's confidence like word-of-mouth recommendations.

Although viral marketing has always been important, the modern era of

Internet marketing has given it a whole new meaning. Have you ever bought a book after hearing from a friend that it was good to read? Did you end up reading it? Or, how many times have you gone to a restaurant on someone else's recommendation? You already know what viral marketing is if you have done these things. When a user tells someone in their network about a product, that's called viral marketing.

Why is viral marketing so relevant to our subject matter? This is due to the fact that viral marketing is both the most effective and cost-effective method for attempting to monetize something. Consider this: the likelihood of acquiring a new

customer is significantly increased when someone recommends your company to a person they know. If you know someone who uses and recommends something, don't you become more interested in it? That's how it works for everyone.

However, the business you get is not the most important thing. It's the self-assurance it gives you. When you are aware that people are not only purchasing your product but also actively promoting it to others, you know you are doing something right. You are motivated to do better as a result of the positive feedback and recommendations you are receiving.

So, where can you promote your products virally? You should

absolutely do it on your blog. Post frequently there. Visitors will arrive. Your product will be used by some of them. They will recommend it to others if they like it. Some could make it happen

on the actual blog. Your ego is really fed by this!

You could also make use of social networking websites. You can invite people to join a particular group on the majority of social networking websites. You might form a group for your own company. Make calls here. Everyone in the community learns about your product when some of them use it and start recommending it. The most important thing is that you learn about it as well. You become quite

content with the course of events. You are not only making money, but you have also created a large number of content customers who are certain to recommend your product to others.

Because due to one version rate is the highest here, viral marketing is very effective however, the fact that interested individuals recommend your product to others who might also be interested is an additional important aspect of this strategy. As a result, your niche begins to expand further.

CHAPTER EIGHT

Building Your Battalion of Interested People

When you have a large group of people who are impressed with your product and help you sell it to more people through referrals or more, you know you're on the right track.

Building Your Team of Interested People It makes perfect sense that if you have a large group of people who will help you promote your product, you will have a much better chance of making money from it. You can accomplish this in a very

straightforward manner thanks to the numerous instruments that the Internet provides.

Keep in mind that confidence naturally develops when you work with a large group of like-minded individuals. These people are your security net; You become more motivated when you see them promoting your product. So, how do you start to gather this group of people? Lead generation is one approach that can be taken in this direction. Obtaining the contact information of people who are even remotely interested in your product or service is known as lead generation. Now, there are other ways to do it, but one of the cheapest and most common is to

give people free things like eBooks or subscriptions to newsletters. You could advertise these giveaways and provide a download link on your blog page itself. However, they will not be able to directly access the giveaway page via this download link. They'll be taken to a squeeze page, where they'll be asked for their email addresses. Because they will receive something for free in exchange, people won't mind giving their email addresses. After that, you'll have access to these email addresses, which you can use to educate people about your company in a variety of ways.

It is your responsibility to keep providing them with high-quality information after they join your list.

Your newsletters, eBooks, or emails may make them so impressed that they buy your product. They join your formidable battalion when they like that. They won't mind if you tell other people about your product.

When it comes to monetizing your content, the same holds. You could ask readers to subscribe to your feeds after they read your content. They will automatically be informed whenever you update the content if they do that. They will

visit again.

They might join the group of people who admire you. These people will then recommend you to other people, which you can speed up by offering them an incentive like a free

subscription or eBook, for example. Now your army is working. It is extending the reach of your business concept.

CHAPTER NINE

Setup of Residual Income Monetization

Streams should never be done once. It must be a consistent effort that can continue to bring in money.

You can monetize something multiple times if you can do so once.

This is a very significant fact, and it is even more significant on the Internet, where it is extremely common to generate multiple streams of income.

This is rooted in the idea of residual cash. Let's first examine what residual money is. Money that keeps coming in for something you did once is called residual money. Retained income is earned by authors who receive royalties for their works.

After completing the book once, they continue to receive royalties from its sales practically throughout their entire lives.

You could carry out the same actions online. You could, for instance, write an eBook and market it on several different Internet sites. This eBook could be about something you want to make money from, like how to play the right way on a six-string guitar. You could

write with authority and promote it on your blog and other affiliate websites.

People will soon begin downloading the eBook in exchange for payment, and as the stream of viral marketing begins to flow, you will also begin receiving additional funds generated for your purposes.

There is a steady stream of residual monetization on the Internet for each blog, website, and article that is created. You can simply dig into these, which are your virtual footprints, and continue to earn money. You must have heard of multimillionaire Internet marketers.

However, they didn't achieve this by constantly exerting effort on every task.

They achieved this by monetizing their expertise and knowledge. Their marketing efforts, which were significant and kept the ball rolling, were one-time.

Therefore, you must spread yourself as widely as possible on the Internet. Learn more about the idea of link exchange and affiliate marketing. You can spread yourself thin across a larger virtual surface in this way. This is what will draw more people to what you're trying to sell and provide you with a steady income that you can be proud of.

CHAPTER TEN

Realizing the Power of "I Can"

Without confidence in one's abilities, it is impossible to profit from the world's most popular product.

Everything is rooted in confidence.

Even if you were given the world's best-selling product and told to make money from it, you wouldn't be able to do so if you weren't sure about it.

Worldwide, numerous McDonald's and Taco Bell franchises have failed.

How come they failed? Was it because the product hadn't yet demonstrated its worth? The sellers'

lack of confidence was the real reason.

You are the source of every success. We have completely failed so far. Being in the right place at the right time is something we talk about. All right, but how could you ever succeed if you didn't seize the opportunity when it came your way? Realizing and having faith in our abilities are the keys to success. We must turn the notion of debility into possibility and avoid it.

Therefore, you can profit from the slogans you write so well. The cakes you bake can be sold for money. Your knowledge of hydraulic screws can help you make money. Your love of Lost can help you make money.

All you have to do is believe you can profit from these opportunities.

Start by imagining that there are people out there who want or, more likely, need to be aware of or possess what it is that you are attempting to monetize. You gain confidence when you are completely convinced that there is a real market. You are aware that you only need to provide the individuals with the goods now that they are prepared.

There are numerous online ways to give. The Internet can bring people in this particular group closer to you. You become so extremely confident about everything thanks to the Internet.

Therefore, explore the power of "I can. "It pushes you to make money.

CHAPTER ELEVEN

Conclusion

If you put your mind to it, you can make money from scrap and junk. It is also possible to monetize something multiple times if it has real value.

You must first instill in yourself the self-assurance that you are capable of doing that.

That may have already taken place.

Best of luck to you!

www.ingramcontent.com/pod-product-compliance
Lightning Source LLC
LaVergne TN
LVHW052105160826
845678LV00015B/3365

* 9 7 9 8 3 5 6 0 3 3 2 3 0 *